TURTLES
AS A NEW PET

CONTENTS

Chelonians—Their Past and Present, 2
Tortoises, 6
Aquatic Turtles, 30
Health Problems, 52
Index, 64

Photos by William B. Allen Jr., Dr. Herbert R. Axelrod, Dr. Warren Burgess, Dr. Guido Dingerkus, Isabelle Francais, M. Freiberg, K. Gillett, Michael Gilroy, Burkhard Kahl, Ken Lucas, Russell Mittermeier, K.T. Nemuras, Hans Peter, Dr. Peter C.H. Pritchard, H. Reinhard, Mervin F. Roberts, P. Schauenberg, Harald Schultz, Robert S. Simmons, John Visser, Jeff Wines, H. Zimmermann.

Painted Turtle
(*Chrysemys picta*).
Photo by Dr. Herbert
R. Axelrod.

Distributed in the UNITED STATES by T.F.H. Publications, Inc., One T.F.H. Plaza, Neptune City, NJ 07753; in CANADA to the Pet Trade by H & L Pet Supplies Inc., 27 Kingston Crescent, Kitchener, Ontario N2B 2T6; Rolf C. Hagen Ltd., 3225 Sartelon Street, Montreal 382 Quebec; in CANADA to the Book Trade by Macmillan of Canada (A Division of Canada Publishing Corporation), 164 Commander Boulevard, Agincourt, Ontario M1S 3C7; in ENGLAND by T.F.H. Publications, The Spinney, Parklands, Portsmouth PO7 6AR; in AUSTRALIA AND THE SOUTH PACIFIC by T.F.H. (Australia) Pty. Ltd., Box 149, Brookvale 2100 N.S.W., Australia; in NEW ZEALAND by Ross Haines & Son, Ltd., 82 D Elizabeth Knox Place, Panmure, Auckland, New Zealand; in the PHILIPPINES by Bio-Research, 5 Lippay Street, San Lorenzo Village, Makati, Rizal; in SOUTH AFRICA by Multipet Pty. Ltd., P.O. Box 35347, Northway, 4065, South Africa. Published by T.F.H. Publications, Inc. Manufactured in the United States of America by T.F.H. Publications, Inc.

Chelonians — Their Past and Present

About 200 million years ago, in the geological period referred to as the Triassic, the ancestors of the order Chelonia, which comprises the entire group known as turtles, terrapins and tortoises, were present on the earth alongside the dinosaurs. The turtle called *Triassochelys* from this period was indeed similar in appearance to those seen today, and grew to a size of at least 90 cm. (3 ft.), although it differed from modern turtles by possessing teeth. Subsequently, seventy million years later, in the seas of the Cretaceous period, there were giant turtles larger than any alive today, which reached a length of about 3.3 m. (11 ft.) and were 3.6 m. (12 ft.) in diameter at their broadest point.

This group of reptiles, collectively known as chelonians and characterized by their protective shells, survived the dramatic changes which saw the extinction of the dinosaurs. Today, although reduced both in size and numbers,

Western Painted Turtle (*Chrysemys picta belli*).

about two hundred species still remain, being concentrated in the warmer areas of the world.

The largest land members of the order today are the giant tortoises (*Geochelone elephantopus* and *G. gigantea*), confined to the Galapagos Islands off the western coast of northern South America and the Aldabras and Seychelles in the Indian Ocean. Their eggs are about the same size as those of domestic chickens and the hatchlings take a minimum period of about forty years, and perhaps longer, to achieve their full size. They can grow to 1.5 m (5 ft.) overall and may weigh 255 kg (550 lbs). Some individual giant tortoises may have lived for more than 150 years, but figures generally are unreliable because the original age of these creatures is unknown.

Nomenclature and Characteristics

The term *chelonian* is often applied to members of this

Galapagos Giant Tortoise (*Geochelone elephantopus*).

3

order, which comprises the reptiles variously known as tortoises, terrapins and turtles. *Tortoises* are terrestrial turtles belonging to the family Testudinidae. The description *terrapin*, first coined by early American settlers for chelonians which lived in brackish water, is now often used in Europe for all species of freshwater chelonian. The term turtle is thus confined in Europe solely to marine species, such as the Leatherback (*Dermochelys coriacea*), which do not fall within the scope of this book, while the land forms are known as *tortoises*. In America most people call the whole group "turtles," and still restrict the name "terrapin" to a single edible coastal species, the Diamondback Terrapin. The

A pair of Red-eared Turtles (*Chrysemys scripta elegans*).

shell of all chelonians, enclosing their bodies except for the head, tail and limbs, sets them apart from all other vertebrates. The upper surface, known as the *carapace*, is generally domed in tortoises and flattened to reduce water resistance in the case of primarily aquatic chelonians. The *carapace* is joined along the sides of the body to the lower half of the shell, referred to as the *plastron*.

Chelonians have some features in common with birds, but, as a reptilian group, they are more closely related to crocodiles than to snakes or lizards. Their jaws lack teeth, even though some species are voracious predators, and they reproduce by laying eggs, although their shells are less calcareous than those of birds. Like other reptiles, they do not have the ability to control their body temperature directly, and so are regarded popularly as being cold-blooded. This is something of a misnomer though, because they can be killed very rapidly by exposure to high temperatures outside their natural range. In fact, temperature is a crucial factor in keeping all reptiles successfully in captivity.

5

Tortoises

The availability of the species covered in this chapter varies from country to country, but the majority can be acquired in the United States. Elsewhere, specifically in Europe, there are restrictions on the movement of these chelonians, notably the following, more hardy species sometimes known as just "Greek" tortoises. Their distribution is, in fact, much wider and several distinct species are recognized.

The Moorish or Mediterranean Spur-Thighed Tortoise (*Testudo graeca*) is easily distinguished by the presence of the so-called *spurs* or *tubercles*. These are located on the insides of both hind thighs between the top of the hind legs and the tail. The spurs are more prominent in some individuals than others but are always unmistakable. There are also other minor anatomical distinguishing features such as the fact that the supracaudal shield, located directly above the tail, is not divided.

These tortoises have a wide range throughout the countries bordering the Mediterranean Sea, extending from Spain through to Turkey and round to Tunisia and Morocco in North Africa. There is, perhaps not surprisingly therefore, some variation in their coloration, and no two individuals appear identical in this respect. Their shell markings are a mixture of black blotches on a brownish yellow background while their skin color can vary from ochre to black. Specimens may reach up to 30 cm. (1 ft.) in size. As with all such measurements quoted for chelonians, this refers to the length of the carapace, measured in a straight line across the center of the shell.

Another species which is quite often imported is the true Greek or Hermann's Tortoise (*T. hermanni*). This form occurs along the northern coast of the Mediterranean, including parts of France, the islands of Corsica, Sardinia and Sicily, and Yugoslavia. It is

not found in North Africa. Hermann's Tortoise lacks the spurs present in the previous species and has a longer, narrower tail which ends in a point. In addition, the supracaudal shield is divided into two parts. Their shells often appear smoother than those of Spur-thighed Tortoises.

The only species confined to Greece is the Margined Tortoise (*T. marginata*). The carapace provides the means of recognizing this variety, as the marginal shields, extending backwards over the legs, are enlarged and form a flange with serrated edges. The supracaudal shield is not split into two, and there are no spurs on the hind legs. The shell color is generally darker on the carapace and yellowish underneath, with black triangular-shaped patches on each shield of the plastron. Like the preceding species it may reach a size of about 30 cm. (12 in.).

Selecting a Healthy Specimen

Watch the tortoises on offer for a few moments before carrying out a closer examination. Any which sit with their heads lying flat out and appear relatively inert are likely to be unhealthy, unless their surroundings are relatively

Ventral view of a young Mexican Forest Turtle (*Rhinoclemmys pulcherrima*).

Hatchling Tropical Slider (*Chrysemys dorbigni*).

cold. A healthy tortoise will have its eyes open and should withdraw quickly into its shell when first approached at close quarters. The condition of its shell is relatively unimportant, providing there is no major damage visible. Check, in the case of young tortoises, however, to ensure that it is not very soft. This sign is indicative of a nutritional disorder.

Picking up the tortoise will provide further clues as to its state of health. Whenever handling a tortoise, especially one that is not used to being picked up, the rear end should be held away from clothing as it may respond by voiding fluid and feces. People who deal with tortoises regularly can tell whether an individual is underweight, but for the inexperienced, comparison with others in a group is useful.

A healthy tortoise will often struggle when handled, moving its legs back and forth fiercely. This gives an opportunity to examine them particularly for any cuts which can become infected if left untreated. The nails on the claws should also be checked, in case they will need to be cut later. Depending on the dealer, the tortoise may still have some ticks sticking to its body, but these parasites are not generally a significant problem as they can be easily removed.

At this stage, it is convenient to take a closer look at the head as well. The eyes and nose should be free from any discharge, although a small quantity of mucus at the corner of the eyes of a tortoise which otherwise appears healthy need not give undue cause for concern. If the eyes are sunken and encircled with a narrow gap, this is a sign of malnutrition and probably dehydration as well.

The mouth should appear clean around the mandibles. Opening the jaws is a difficult procedure and requires care, but if it is possible, then the interior will reveal the surprisingly fleshy pink tongue within. There must not be any signs of ulceration or infection inside the mouth, as such complaints are difficult to treat successfully and can spread to other tortoises.

Housing and Care

The accommodation required for these tortoises will be influenced by the weather conditions in the area concerned, and certainly some provision must be made to keep them indoors when the weather is wet or cold. It is preferable to purchase a tortoise in the spring, so that it has the whole summer to settle in its new surroundings. It should then be possible to hibernate the reptile for at least part of the winter, whereas a tortoise obtained toward the latter part of the summer may not have eaten

Malayan Snail-eating Turtle (*Malayemys subtrijuga*). Due to its diet, which mainly consists of molluscs, this species is very difficult to keep in captivity.

False Map Turtle, *Graptemys pseudogeographica.* The bumps on its carapace give this species its alternative name—Sawback.

sufficiently well to survive a period of enforced dormancy. As a result, such tortoises should be kept awake indoors and fed normally through the winter.

Size is also significant, since smaller tortoises are less hardy than their larger counterparts, and those under about 12.5 cm. (5 in.) in length should not be hibernated for long periods. It is not essential for a tortoise to hibernate, however, so that if the resulting complications are considered beforehand, then size need not be an important factor in selecting an individual.

Most people keep their tortoises outside during the day in summertime when the weather is fine. It should be remembered, however, that tortoises are capable not only of digging, but also of climbing at least their own height. They are nomadic creatures by nature and wander freely, being no respecters of flower beds or their contents.

Various methods have therefore been used to restrict a tortoise's domain. It is extremely cruel to tether these reptiles, by whatever means. Tying a tortoise by its leg will soon cause the cord to cut into the flesh and result in severe injury and even possibly loss of the limb. Attempts at drilling a hole in the rear marginal shields for a tether are equally barbaric, apart from being quite unnecessary.

Constructing a Run

A simple wooden run or

11

barrier is quite effective in restraining a tortoise if it cannot be allowed to roam free in the garden. A solid partition is always preferable to using wire netting as some individuals will persistently endeavor to get through the mesh and may injure themselves as a result. As a guide, the height of the run needs to be twice the size of the largest tortoise to prevent it from climbing out.

The run should be as large as possible, and must include a suitable house where the reptile can retreat during the day if the weather turns bad. This need not be an expensive structure, merely draft-proof and dry with a cover of roofing felt on the roof, which should be removable. Alternatively, a corner of the run can have a covering of plastic sheeting, with a piece of paneling built onto the run to provide a third side for the structure. This is most convenient if the run is being moved regularly. The shelter should have a minimum floor area of 900 sq. cm. (1 sq. ft.), with a wide entrance to allow the tortoise to move in and out freely.

Tortoises are creatures of habit and, having been placed inside several times, most will readily adopt the shelter. Newspaper cut into narrow strips is the most suitable bedding material for the interior of the shelter and should be changed at quite frequent intervals. Straw often has sharp protruding ends, which can injure the eyes, while hay, especially if it is damp, is a potentially dangerous source of fungal spores which can lead to respiratory infections.

Locating the Run

Tortoises require a warm, dry location in the garden, but they must also be able to find some protection from the sun on hot days. A well-drained piece of lawn is probably most suitable as a starting point, since the tortoise will then be able to forage for food as well.

The run may either be established in this position or moved at intervals to allow the grass to recover. The house can be set on bricks protruding about 7.5 cm. (3 in.) above ground level in the center of the run so that the tortoise can move around freely without the risk of getting caught between the sides of the house and

European Pond Turtle (*Emys orbicularis*). This species was once prized in Europe as a Lenten delicacy.

13

perimeter. A suitable ramp gives access to the raised house, while a water bowl should be sunk into the ground with its rim just protruding above the surface. This will help to prevent debris falling into the bowl and furthermore it cannot be tipped over by accident. A paving slab included in the run is useful so that the tortoise has access to a hard surface, which should help to prevent its claws becoming overgrown. Keeping them exclusively on such a surface is not to be recommended, however, as it may lead to sores developing on the feet and even excessive wear on the plastron. It will also enjoy basking here as the slab will hold the sun's heat.

The main drawback of a run kept in one location is that ultimately the lawn will suffer, especially under the pet house, where the grass will soon turn yellow and die off. From the tortoise's viewpoint, there is an increased risk of parasitic worm infections spreading from one member of a group to another if they are kept together on a restricted piece of ground. Cleanliness will

certainly help to reduce this problem, but it is not easy to clean up thoroughly on a grass floor. The microscopic worm eggs are likely to be washed out of the feces by water and pass down into the grass. Infection occurs subsequently when the tortoise feeds on contaminated herbage.

The accommodation itself will need to be inspected daily, in case the tortoise starts to burrow underneath. Their front feet are well-adapted for powerful digging. With a permanent run, it is useful to set a course of bricks below ground around the perimeter to deter the tortoise from burrowing out, and then place the run on top of this layer.

Indoor Accommodation

This aspect of care is neglected by many owners, but it is especially important during bad weather for encouraging an individual to keep up its appetite. Indoors, an area with an electrical outlet nearby for a light should be set aside for the tortoises. They will need to be confined again in a pen, with the floor area

covered in a thick layer of newspaper, perhaps with a plastic sheet underneath. Good hygiene is obviously important, and as always, children and other pets such as dogs must not be allowed to come into contact with the tortoise's droppings.

A light source suspended out of reach over the pen should be left on during the day. This will also give out some heat and encourage the tortoise to eat. For those which are overwintered inside, however, a natural light bulb will be an essential piece of equipment.

Feeding

All the preceding species of tortoise are essentially vegetarian, and so cannot be expected to eat garden pests such as slugs and snails. They will sometimes take a little lean minced meat, canned cat food or even mynah bird pellets soaked in water, which all provide useful variety in the diet. Such animal protein is a better source of the essential amino acids necessary for health and growth than is protein derived from plants. Tortoises do have individual food preferences and, within

Wood Turtle (*Clemmys insculpta*). Members of this species feed mainly on snails and worms, but occasionally they will take fruit and other plants.

15

Malayan Box Turtle (*Cuora amboinensis*). Box Turtles are basically carnivorous; they are hardy and make good pets for the aqua-terrarium.

Painted Turtle (*Chrysemys picta dorsalis*). Painted Turtles and Sliders start out as carnivores but take increasing amounts of vegetation as they grow larger in size.

reason, can be fed accordingly. Some variety, however, is to be recommended and indeed, their tastes often change as the summer progresses. This may also be a reflection of the amount of lignin in the plants themselves, as older, tougher leaves are usually less acceptable than more succulent items.

It is not an expensive undertaking to feed a tortoise during the summer months. The reptiles themselves will forage on a lawn, eating a variety of weeds, including plantain leaves, clover and chickweed. Dandelion leaves and flowers are a particular favorite and often accepted by those which refuse other foods. Cultivated crops, such as lettuce and tomatoes cut up into pieces, are popular, while soft fruits such as plums and cherries, the stones of which have been removed beforehand, can also be fed. Strawberries in season, peas and apples are other possible alternatives.

Avoid Contamination

The main concerns when feeding are that the food is fresh and free from possible contamination, especially by chemical sprays. Indeed, no tortoise should be allowed on grass which has been recently treated with a weedkiller. Fruit and green food should be washed before feeding, especially if they have been purchased.

Food Supplements

Calcium is particularly important for a tortoise's shell and bones, and since the levels in plants are relatively low, it is useful to supplement this vital mineral by scraping cuttlefish bone over the food once or twice a week. A mixed mineral and vitamin powder, obtainable from pet stores, can also be given simply, as it will stick readily to damp food. Only small quantities of such supplements are required as indicated on the pack; in fact, an excess can be harmful over a period of time.

Water

Water should always be available even if the tortoises do not appear to drink a

European Tortoise munching on lettuce. Although it may be a favorite of your pet, lettuce is low in nutritional value and should not be a dietary staple.

great deal. The container must not be too deep or if one falls in and cannot get out, it may well drown. Plastic plant trays make the most suitable water pots for tortoises. The contents will need to be changed daily.

Daily Management

Tortoises, unfortunately, may appeal to those who are seeking a pet but lack the sense of responsibility which should be an integral part of ownership. While these reptiles are certainly not as demanding as other pets (possibly because they are not vocal), tortoises do require daily attention and should never be left to fend for themselves.

Overnight

It is advisable to bring the reptiles in at night, housing them in boxes lined with paper and filled with strips of newspaper. This will protect them from sudden unexpected changes in the weather and possible predators such as any prowling foxes, dogs or cats in the neighborhood. The tortoises can then be placed outside again the following morning once the sun has begun to evaporate the previous night's dew. On wet days or when the temperature is below about 15°C. (60°F.), they will need to be kept inside until the weather improves.

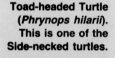

Toad-headed Turtle (*Phrynops hilarii*). This is one of the Side-necked turtles.

Feeding Times

Tortoises are browsing creatures, preferring to nibble at one plant and then move on to the next, rather than consuming a large quantity of vegetation in one place. This behavior is reflected in their captive feeding habits and can be particularly infuriating if they have progressed along a line of lettuce or bean seedlings in this manner, just nibbling off the main shoots. Considering their instincts, it is therefore preferable to offer them smaller quantities of food twice or three times a day, rather than giving just one large meal.

Feeding should be carried out in the same place at about the same time each day, so the tortoises learn to expect their food. This is obviously more critical for those which are ranging over a garden rather than being kept in a pen.

Shell Care

During the summer months, olive oil can be rubbed into the tortoise's shell at weekly intervals. It is conveniently applied on cotton wool or a paper tissue. Apart from

American River Turtle (*Podocnemis erythrocephala*).

improving the condition and appearance of the shell, the oil helps to keep the tortoise dry if it is caught in a heavy downpour. Most tortoises dislike rain, although some will sit quite contentedly in a shallow bowl of water during hot weather. This presumably is a means of keeping cool.

Management of Newly Imported Tortoises

The first two years in their new surroundings are a

19

crucial period for all imported tortoises, and mortality is at its highest during this time. Most deaths can be traced back, however, to neglect on the part of their owners.

Maintain a Healthy Appetite

It is vital to check that the creature is eating regularly. A healthy average-sized tortoise should consume a minimum of approximately half a lettuce head or its equivalent a day. One that merely nibbles at its food and eats only a couple of dandelion leaves over several days requires further attention. A few newly imported tortoises refuse wet food but will consume unwashed greenstuff quite readily.

The caring owner will endeavor to weigh the tortoise at regular intervals after purchase and keep a log so that changes and, it is to be hoped, increases in weight can be noted. Placing the reptile in a strong carrier bag is perhaps the most suitable method of carrying out this procedure.

Newly imported tortoises are particularly prone to

chills in the cooler, damp summers and should not be allowed out in inclement weather. They will refuse food if kept under such conditions, and loss of appetite should be avoided at all costs. One of the main problems facing the owner is to get the tortoise eating well before hibernation.

Hibernation

Tortoises hibernate naturally in the wild state when the temperature falls and food is likely to be in short supply. Such behavior is not confined exclusively to chelonians, but is seen in a variety of other animal species, ranging from snakes to squirrels. The body processes of the creature are slowed almost to a standstill, and it becomes completely inert. In the case of an American ground squirrel for example, its heartbeat falls from about three hundred beats a minute down to as few as five.

The time when hibernation commences will vary each year, according to the weather. During a mild fall, the tortoises may remain active until well into October, but some years they will become torpid as early as September. Apart from losing interest in their food, they are inactive except for attempting to dig themselves into the ground of their enclosure.

In the wild, tortoises bury themselves completely, and they can survive like this until the warmth of the following spring revives them.

The Container

When the tortoise appears ready for hibernation, therefore, assuming it is both healthy and of sufficient size and weight, it should be placed in a cardboard box packed with thin strips of paper into which it can burrow. This box should then be placed in a second, larger container and the sides packed round with peat, newspaper or styrofoam blocks which should help to provide some insulation.

Storing

Once the top has been wired over with netting, the box must be stored in a frost-free environment for the duration of the winter. The temperature should be low and remain as constant as possible, because if it rises sharply the tortoise will emerge prematurely from hibernation, and this may lead to problems. An unheated room away from hot water pipes is ideal, holding a temperature between 5°-10°C. (40-50°F.).

All tortoises should be left alone after they have begun hibernating, and there is no need to do more than glance at the box each week just to check they have not been drawn out of their slumber by a warm spell. From springtime onward as a general rule, the reptiles will wake from their winter hibernation and can be put outside for short periods when the sun is shining and

A group of Yellow-spotted Amazon Turtle (*Podocnemis unifilis*) hatchlings.

the weather is warm.

Management After Hibernation

For several weeks after hibernation these creatures require careful management. As always, they must not be exposed to frost or damp conditions. A wide selection of foodstuffs should be offered to tempt their appetites.

When it first emerges from hibernation, the tortoise is likely to be sluggish and may not eat for several days. Many will drink freely at this stage to replace the fluid lost during hibernation, and water must be provided within easy reach. A soluble multi-vitamin preparation can be administered via the drinking water, and should help to stimulate the tortoise's appetite.

If the tortoise appears to be having difficulty in opening its eyes, these can be bathed gently, using wet cotton wool. Alternatively, immerse the tortoise in a shallow bath. This should ensure that both its eyes and nostrils are clean.

Growth and Aging

The growth rate of young tortoises appears to be a very variable characteristic. Some gain weight quickly, while others which appear equally healthy develop at a much slower rate. It is likely that by about two years of age the tortoise will weigh approximately 230 g. (8 oz.).

It is impossible to correlate the age of a specimen with the number of "growth rings" present on the shields of the carapace. The rearing of young tortoises confirms that these will develop before the age of one year is obtained. If the rate of growth is artificially fast, with a high level of protein present in the diet, then deformed growth of the carapace may occur, creating a typically knobbed rather than smooth appearance. Tortoises grow for much of their lives, with maturity being reached probably during their eighth year in the case of the European species. In very old specimens, as in hatchlings, the shell is essentially smooth as the growth rings have been worn away.

Other Species

Various tropical tortoises are occasionally available, including the Red-footed Tortoise (*Geochelone carbonaria*), which occurs over a wide area of South America. The orange-red markings seen in young specimens become less evident in older individuals. Like the closely-related Yellow-footed species (*Geochelone denticulata*), this is potentially a large tortoise whose carapace can measure 42.5 cm. (17 in.) or more in length. They are forest-dwelling tortoises, and tend to dislike bright conditions, preferring subdued lighting. It is not possible to keep them outside unless the weather is very mild, as they need a temperature in excess of 20°C. (70°F.), proving even less hardy than their European counterparts and readily succumbing to respiratory ailments when kept under damp, cold conditions.

The third South American species is the Argentine or Chaco tortoise (*Geochelone chilensis*), which is found in relatively arid surroundings. Other closely related forms have recently been described from Argentina as well. These tortoises, unlike the

Scorpion Mud Turtle (*Kinosternon scorpioides*). This species is the largest of the Mud Turtles.

previous two species, feed largely on vegetation, even cacti, in the wild state, although they will also take fruit like their northern counterparts.

The Leopard Tortoise (*Geochelone pardalis*) found over much of Africa is another essentially herbivorous species. It can grow to 60 cm. (2 ft.) and has a proportionately large appetite. The carapace markings of this species are said to resemble the skin of a leopard in appearance, although older individuals tend to have duller markings. These tortoises delight in basking in hot sunlight. The African Hingeback Tortoises, living naturally in forested areas, prefer more shaded conditions. All three species are similar in appearance and are characterized by their hinged plastrons which enable them to retreat into their shells with their hindlimbs fully protected. Bell's Hingeback (*Kinixys belliani*) is the most common species, showing a wide range of markings over its extensive distribution through much of Africa. It has a smooth edge to its

carapace, whereas the marginal shields of the Eroded Hingeback (*Kinixys erosa*) are serrated. Home's Hingeback (*Kinixys homeana*) is similar in appearance, but while the carapace of the Eroded follows a simple curve at its rear, that of Home's falls almost vertically.

Hingebacks tend to consume relatively large quantities of water, and partial immersion in a bowl may subsequently encourage a reluctant individual to start feeding. The forest species in particular tend to prefer fruits and will readily take tomatoes cut into pieces. Males can be recognized by their significantly longer tails compared with females. Another African tortoise, less often seen, is the relatively large and dull Spurred Tortoise (*Geochelone sulcata*), which feeds primarily on herbage rather than fruit. This species can grow bigger than the Leopard and has prominent spurs on both thighs.

Perhaps the most unusual species, discovered as recently as 1920 in East Africa, is the Pancake Tortoise (*Malacochersus tornieri*) with its flattened carapace being more typical of an aquatic turtle. The shell of this species is naturally soft, and for protection these tortoises depend on the speed of their legs to reach the safety of cracks and crevices in the rocky areas where they occur.

No tortoises occur in Australia and relatively few Asiatic species are available. Perhaps the most common is the Yellow Tortoise (*Geochelone elongata*). It is also known as the Elongated Tortoise because of its body shape. The markings in this species are variable, and some individuals have

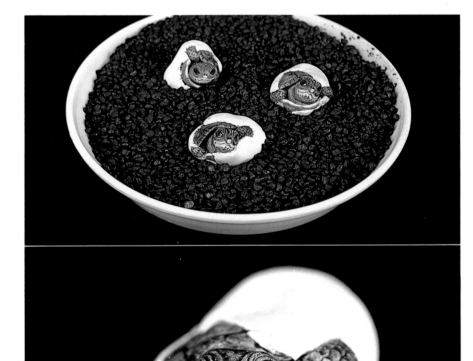

Eastern Box Turtles (*Terrapene carolina*) on their way out.

Close-up of an egg callus on an Eastern Box Turtle. The egg callus aids the youngster in opening the shell; it drops off soon after hatching.

25

heavily pigmented carapaces. They require a high proportion of fruit in their diet. Like other species in this section, they should not be hibernated, which can make feeding during the winter months an expensive consideration.

Two other Asiatic tortoises, the Brown (*Geochelone emys*), which builds a domed nest which the female protects for a short period after laying her eggs, and the striking, relatively small Starred Tortoise (*Geochelone elegans*), may occasionally be available.

In North America, there are four species of tortoise which all belong to the genus *Gopherus*. Where the winters are cold, gopher tortoises burrow to survive the

inhospitable weather, using their powerful front feet for this purpose. Their tunnels may reach a length of 7.5 m. (25 ft.), and there is one on record which extended 14.25 m (47½ ft.) from the entrance. They end in a chamber which may be lined with some form of vegetation.

These burrows provide sanctuary for a wide variety of other animals and have proved a major reason for the decline in the numbers of gopher tortoises. Several species of snake may be found in their burrows, including Diamondback Rattlesnakes (*Crotalus adamanteus*), and gassing such reptiles also kills the tortoises. Many of these chelonians succumb to passing traffic on highways. Through most of their range, which extends into Mexico, they are protected. In view of their burrowing habits, gophers are not the easiest species to maintain successfully under captive conditions.

Box Turtles

The box turtles are much easier to cater to than the gopher tortoises. They are not true tortoises, as they belong to the aquatic family Emydidae, but have many adaptations for living on land most of their lives. Four species with many local variants are recognized, and again their distribution extends down into Mexico. The Eastern or Common Box Turtle (*Terrapene carolina*) ranges down the eastern side of the USA and occurs in various distinct forms, with the Florida race (*Terrapene carolina bauri*) being perhaps the most striking. It usually has three toes on its hind limbs; the Three-toed Box Turtle (*Terrapene carolina triunguis*), which occurs further west sometimes has four toes, in spite of its name, so this characteristic is not a reliable identification feature. Box turtles tend to be relatively small, being around 12.5 cm. (5 in.) in carapace length. They are also reputed to be long-lived, and some individuals may live for over a century.

The characteristic feature of these turtles is their hinged plastron, which enables them to withdraw completely into their shells. If a large specimen closes up suddenly, trapping a finger in the process, it can be very painful. They can generally be sexed without difficulty because males have red eyes while those of females are brown, but exceptions to this rule have been recorded. Males also have deeply concave plastral lobes.

These chelonians appear to occupy an intermediate position between tortoises and aquatic turtles. Although they live on land, they tend to prefer damp conditions and must always be provided with a shallow bowl of water in which they can sit with their heads out.

Box turtles generally do not like bright sunlight and require adequate shade in hot weather. After a rain shower or in the early morning dew, however, they become very active,

Murray River Turtle (*Emydura macquari*) coming up for air. This species is one of the Australian Short-necked Turtles.

searching for their prey. These turtles are largely carnivorous. Those which refuse meat or fish will often accept live food such as earthworms and snails. Some vegetable matter, such as tomatoes, will also be accepted.

In view of their relatively small size, box turtles are suitable to be kept in an indoor vivarium. They can be allowed to hibernate for a short period during the winter if they have been feeding well through the previous year. Mating in the wild takes place shortly after the turtles emerge from hibernation, with about five eggs forming a typical clutch. Egg-laying commonly occurs during the months of June and July, normally toward evening.

The Ornate Box Turtle (*Terrapene ornata*) is the only other species found in the United States and overlaps through part of its range with the Common Box Turtle, which it closely resembles. The presence of yellow stripes on the plastron can prove a distinguishing feature of the Ornate Box Turtle. Both these species range into Mexico, where two other box turtles (*Terrapene coahuila* and *Terrapene nelsoni*) also occur, although these appear relatively localized. They should not be confused with the more aquatic *Cuora* species, also known as box turtles, originating from Asia.

Opposite top: Hermann's Tortoise hatchlings awaiting a new arrival. This species is also known as the Greek Tortoise. *Opposite bottom:* Hermann's Tortoise snacking on a plant. Be sure that all plants are safe before you give them to your pet.

Hawksbill Turtle (*Eretmochelys imbricata*).

Aquatic Turtles

Aquatic turtles, like tortoises, have a wide distribution throughout the warmer regions of the world. Those most commonly kept in captivity, however, originate from North America and Europe. The export of Australian species is not permitted, while African turtles and those from South America are rarely available.

A Selection of Species

Pond turtles, *Emys* and allies, are among the hardiest of the freshwater chelonians and occur in both Europe and North America. The European form *Emys orbicularis* is now confined to parts of Poland and Germany in the north, southward to the Mediterranean and Algeria.

In France, European Pond Turtles were valued by farmers during the last century as a means of keeping water troughs free of worms which were thought would otherwise infect their stock. Although the origins of this superstition have been lost, the idea did spread and the poor reptiles were also kept for the same reason in swill buckets used for feeding pigs.

The coloration of this species is very variable through its range and may also change with age. Young European Pond Turtles have a dark brown carapace with a yellow spot on each marginal shield. The plastron is similarly marked but darker, being black in color. As the youngsters grow, characteristic yellow striations and spots appear on the carapace. The remainder of the body is dark, with some yellow coloration. Old specimens, which may reach a length of 17.5 cm. (7 in.), lose much of the yellow on the carapace, which therefore appears dark brown.

The North American Blanding's Turtle (*Emydoidea blandingi*) occurs around the Great Lakes. It is somewhat similar in coloration to the European Pond Turtle but grows to a greater size, reaching 25 cm. (10 in.) in length. The carapace is more domed while the plastron is hinged like that of the box turtle. It is said to be relatively terrestrial in its habits in the wild.

In addition to the Pond Turtle, there are two other European species of aquatic chelonian. The Spanish Turtle (*Mauremys leprosa*) occurs in southern France, Spain and North Africa. Its carapace is dark brown, becoming olive gray in older specimens, with a yellowish plastron. The soft parts are also grayish, with yellow stripes prominent, particularly on the sides of the head and the limbs.

Spanish Turtles may attain a carapace length of about 15 cm. (6 in.) and live naturally in muddy pools, coming out to bask in sunshine. The water in some pools is also populated with a certain species of algae which can enter and grow under the shell shields, even invading the bone in severe cases. This algae gave rise to the specific name *leprosa* for these terrapins, as it causes the shell to resemble that of a leper.

The Caspian Turtle (*Mauremys caspica*) is found

A pair of Texas Sliders (*Chrysemys concinna*) taking a breather. Members of this species are also known as River Cooters.

in the area surrounding the Caspian Sea, extending into Asia. It resembles the Spanish species, but its plastron is black, augmented with yellow patches in the case of an adult, which reaches a maximum size of about 15 cm. (6 in.).

Members of the Genus *Chrysemys*

The Red-eared Turtle (*Chrysemys (Pseudemys) scripta elegans*) occurs in the southeastern states of America, from Missouri and North Carolina to the Gulf of Mexico. It is a popular pet in its homeland and is also exported to Europe in large numbers. Sometimes known as Elegant Sliders, these turtles, with prominent red or orange flashes extending behind their eyes, are unmistakable. The carapace is predominantly green, with yellow markings especially around the edges of the marginal shields; it darkens as the terrapin becomes older. The plastron is completely yellow apart from darker spots or ocelli. This marking pattern is extremely variable among individuals, with some possessing large numbers of such spots, while others have very few.

The Yellow-bellied Turtle (*C. s. scripta*), ranging from central Florida to North Carolina, is a subspecies related to the Red-eared form, but lacks this characteristic marking. It has a predominantly black carapace with brown markings and yellow edging on the marginals. The eyes are green like the previous subspecies, and it also possesses yellow bands on the sides of the face extending to the legs.

Other forms of slider turtles are seen occasionally in petshops, but as their natural distribution ranges from Canada south to Argentina, accurate identification is not always straightforward. In North America alone, six distinct species and sixteen subspecies are recognized, occurring predominantly in central and eastern areas. Some are given local names in the district where they are found, such as the Florida Cooter (*C. floridana*) and the Texas Slider (*C. concinna*). They are also sold sometimes as Hieroglyphic Turtles because of their shell markings. One of the most attractive species is the Red or Orange-bellied slider (*C. rubriventris*) which, as its name suggests, has a red plastron. Precise identification is further

American River Turtle (*Podocnemis erythrocephala*).

33

confused, however, because many of the various forms can interbreed, producing hybrid offspring.

The other major group in this genus comprises the Painted Turtles (*C. picta*), of which four subspecies are recognized. Painted Turtles all have brownish black carapaces edged with red, and yellow markings on the head. Females grow about 5 cm. (2 in.) bigger than their mates, and may reach 17.5 cm. (7 in.) in length. Their

Young Red-eared Slider (*Chrysemys scripta elegans*).

front claws also tend to be shorter than those of males.

Other aquatic turtles are occasionally available, often as hatchlings kept alongside young Red-ears. The majority have similar requirements, however, and so are not as difficult to cater to as many exotic species of tortoise.

Some aquatic turtles have evolved several means of protecting themselves, apart from their shells. Musk turtles of the genus *Sternotherus* produce a most unpleasant odor from glands located close to the edges of marginal shields where the carapace reaches the body. They occur naturally throughout eastern North America, and are also known as Stinkpot Turtles because of their glandular secretions. These chelonians are relatively small, only reaching a length of about 10 cm. (4 in.). Their plastron is very reduced in size, so they are surprisingly mobile, being able to climb to heights of 1.8 m. (6 ft.).

Mud turtles (*Kinosternon* species) produce a similar unpleasant odor and can be distinguished by their hinged plastrons.

Snapping turtles, belonging to the family Chelydridae, are the largest and most aggressive species found in America, and for these reasons tend to be unsuitable as potential pets. They may reach a size of nearly 90 cm. (3 ft.) from head to tail, with a carapace measurement exceeding 45 cm. (18 in.), and often weigh in excess of 15.9 kg. (35 lb.) up to 107 kg. (236 lb.). Adult Snapping Turtles must be handled very carefully because their long necks are extremely flexible and they can inflict a painful bite. They should never be held by the tail, but by grasping the back edge of the carapace firmly. The head must be kept at a safe distance from the handler.

These turtles feed naturally on a range of creatures including fish, waterfowl and even other snappers. Their main enemy in the wild, apart from man, is the American Alligator (*Alligator mississippienis*), which will take even the largest

Desert Tortoise (*Gopherus agassizi*). This species is one of the Gopher Tortoises, named for their habit of burrowing in order to survive cold weather.

snapper. The meat of the snapping turtles used to be highly prized for making soup throughout its range, while their eggs are often fried fresh. They appear to maintain their numbers, however, possibly because they lay a relatively large number of eggs, averaging between twenty and thirty in a clutch. By way of comparison, the Stinkpot usually lays less than five.

A terrapin which was also popular for its meat is the Diamondback (*Malaclemys terrapin*), which inhabits stretches of brackish water. As a result, it is recommended to add some salt to their aquarium surroundings; that sold for marine fish is suitable, but ensure that the solution is much weaker than directed on the pack. There is some evidence to suggest these terrapins may be more at risk from fungal disease if kept just in fresh water.

Pancake or soft-shelled turtles (not to be confused with those suffering from the complaint of the same name) are another aggressive family. The *Trionyx* species have a wider distribution than snapping turtles, being found also in parts of Africa and Asia as well as North America. This group all have soft, leathery carapaces which lack any form of shields. The scientific name *Trionyx* is derived from the presence of only three claws on each foot. Apart from their soft body covering, soft-shelled turtles have long necks which end in pronounced snouts. They are predominantly aquatic and rarely leave the water, remaining buried for long periods under sandy or muddy bottoms.

With their soft shells, they should be kept apart from other chelonians and handled with extra care. As pets, some individuals tame easily, while others remain much shyer, burying themselves at the slightest approach. In a deep tank, a shallow tray filled with mud or sand should be placed on blocks a short distance under the water surface. This will enable the soft-shell turtles to bury themselves and yet extend their heads up to the surface to breathe, as they often do naturally. Gravel is too coarse to use in tanks for these chelonians, as youngsters in particular seem unable to bury themselves satisfactorily. Most appear to resent being moved and have to be fed in their normal tanks.

Another turtle with an unusual shell is the False Map Turtle or Sawback (*Graptemys pseudogeographica*), which has a line of ridges or knobs running down its vertebral shields. Members of this genus are known as map turtles because of the pattern and coloration of the markings on their carapace. Young hatchlings have the most attractive shells in this respect, but become duller as they grow older. Adult females may reach nearly 30 cm. (1 ft.) in length, often being twice the size of their mates.

Red-eared slider (*Chrysemys scripta elegans*).

Obtaining a Turtle

Many petshops stock turtles. In Europe these are particularly of the Red-eared variety. These are hatched commercially in large numbers on turtle farms in the southern United States and freighted to their destinations when perhaps only a few weeks old. Some are also collected in the bayous of Louisiana, but most states generally have restrictions on the capture of chelonians within their boundaries.

In the United States, health laws have made it more difficult to purchase an aquatic turtle, as there are now minimum size limits on what can be sold (usually about 7.5 cm. (3 in.) to 10 cm. (4 in.) minimum carapace length). This means that young sliders, Painted Turtles, and map turtles are no longer sold, and many U.S. petshops no longer carry any aquatic native turtles.

Choosing a Pet Turtle

It is vital to choose an active, healthy turtle in the first instance. The young Red-eared Turtles, often only one and a half inches (3.75 cm) in size, can be difficult to rear successfully. The hardier Pond Turtles and related species are perhaps a better proposition for the novice owner, as they generally maintain their appetite and seem less sensitive to temperature changes.

Selecting a Healthy Turtle

When selecting a young turtle, therefore, only those which are lively and scurry readily into the water should be considered. Any which are sitting on a rock and remain inert with their eyes closed when approached are likely to prove a liability. It is essential that the turtle can open its eyes freely, since without these it will not be able to see to feed. There is an eye disorder which commonly afflicts young Red-eared Turtles. Curing this condition is difficult, but it can be avoided with a sensible diet, as can the problem of soft shell. This is a difficult complaint to recognize in young turtles, since their shells are naturally quite soft, but affected individuals are rarely active.

The shell should also be

inspected for any signs of fungus. This often shows up as a vague halo around the whole body when the turtle is in the water, and should not be confused with green algal growth on the shells of larger individuals. Fungal infections often develop after an injury, so finally the limbs and tail should be checked accordingly. The size of the turtle chosen is largely a matter of personal preference. The smallest specimens may be best avoided, however, because although larger individuals are sometimes reluctant to feed in new surroundings and may not tame so readily, there is a greater chance of acclimatizing these without difficulty.

Housing

A wide variety of tanks are available today, made from glass or plastic, and the majority are quite suitable for housing turtles. A rectangular design is preferable. Circular goldfish bowls should not be used, primarily because of their small size. When purchasing a tank, it should be remembered that young turtles in particular will grow quickly, so a relatively large setup is a sensible investment. A small second tank is useful for feeding purposes and as a temporary home while the main tank is being cleaned.

Most glass tanks are now sealed simply with a rubbery silicone glue around the interior, rather than putty set between the frame and external surfaces. The only disadvantage of this new sealer for large turtles is that their claws can damage the lining if it is not thick enough, resulting in leakages. The problem can be overcome to a great extent by using a thick layer of gravel on the floor of the tank, where the lining is most likely to be breached.

Painted Turtle (*Chrysemys picta dorsalis*) hatchling. This subspecies is sometimes called the Southern Painted Turtle.

Floor Covering

Sand is not recommended as a floor covering, partly because of the abrasive nature of the smaller particles which may cause injury. A further disadvantage is that the water itself often remains cloudy with a scum on the top as the fine particles remain in constant suspension because of the turtle's movements in the tank. Coarse aquarium gravel, purchased from a petshop, is suitable for all turtles except the highly-specialized *Trionyx* species. There should be a minimum covering to a depth of at least 2.5 cm. (1 in.), while 5 cm. (2 in.) is preferable for bigger specimens over 10 cm. (4 in.) in length. Such gravel is now available in a selection of colors, including blue and red, as well as the natural mixture.

Heating

An aquarium heater connected to a thermostat will be necessary to keep the water at the required temperature. It is possible to buy these in one unit or as separate components, and again a variety of models is now marketed. An aquarist shop will give advice on the type required, as the wattage will vary, from a minimum of 50 watts to a total of 300 watts for a tank with a capacity of approximately 163 l (36 gals.). The thermostat is vital to ensure the water in the tank does not become too hot. The setting can usually be altered simply by a small adjustment to a screw in the unit. Great care should be taken over wiring the units correctly and, if in any doubt, the advice of a qualified electrician should be sought.

The temperature of the water will need to be monitored by means of a thermometer. Liquid crystal strips which stick to the outside of the tank and give an easily read digital measure of the water temperature are recommended for this purpose. In a large tank, it is quite useful to have two thermometers at opposite ends, one actually in the water, to check for any temperature differences.

The water circulates effectively, both by convection currents and the action of the filter pump, even when the turtles are out

"In a large tank, it is quite useful to have two thermometers at opposite ends, one actually in the water, to check for any temperature differences."

of the water, and helps to maintain a constant temperature in a large tank. As a general rule, a 10 cm. (4 in.) turtle will require a minimum of 900 sq. cm. (1 sq. ft.) of tank surface space, and pro-rata for a number being kept together.

Lighting

Lighting in the tank is required to serve two major purposes. In the first instance, it helps to keep the air temperature warm for the terrapins when they leave the water. A 40 watt bulb positioned about 15 cm. (6 in.) above the area where they emerge is quite satisfactory. It need only be on for about eight hours during the day; in fact, exposing the turtles to constant light may damage their sight over a period of time.

An aquarium lid complete with light socket is most suitable for turtles, as it allows adequate ventilation. At no time should the tank roof be totally enclosed, as the humidity inside will soon rise to a very high and potentially dangerous level.

For turtles kept inside constantly, natural light is recommended to ensure that they do not suffer from a vitamin D deficiency, which leads to the development of soft shells initially and soon proves fatal if not corrected

Red-footed Tortoise (*Geochelone carbonaria*). This species is quite omnivorous—in other words, it needs a highly varied diet.

rapidly. This essential component of the light spectrum is simply provided by the use of special bulbs.

Setting Up the Tank

The tank should first be washed out at home, as the interior will probably be dirty. Leaving the water to stand in the tank outside for a while is recommended, in case there is an unobserved leak in the seal. This applies particularly to puttied tanks which have been left empty for a period. The gravel itself should be washed thoroughly using a salt solution, and then rinsed through again in a bucket until clean.

Don't try to move the aquarium while it contains water and/or gravel, however, as this will almost certainly result in a broken tank floor or at least major leaks.

Creating a Dry Area

It will also be necessary to obtain some suitable stones to form a dry area where the terrapins can get out of the water to bask under the light. A single block can be used, providing it will protrude only about 1.25 cm. (½ in.) above the water

surface, to enable the young turtles to climb up without difficulty. A smaller second platform just below the surface will facilitate their exit from the water on to the block.

A group of stones can also be used effectively to provide a dry area and serves as a useful means of disguising a filter and possibly a heating unit. They must be stacked securely to prevent accidental damage to the glass tubing around the heater and positioned in such a way that the turtles cannot get trapped in gaps between the stones and sides of the tank. Rough jagged surfaces should be avoided, as these may injure the turtles.

The dry area of the tank must be of sufficient size to allow all the turtles to be out of the water together, if they so wish. Once the stones have been washed thoroughly and rinsed off, it is most convenient to prepare this part of the tank before finally adding the water.

Water

Tap water is quite suitable for the turtles discussed here and can be used directly, rather than having to be left standing for a day or so as is recommended for fish. Pouring it carefully over the stones will help to prevent disruption of the rest of the tank. The water should ideally be about the same temperature as will eventually be required, which is in the region of 23°-29° C. (75°-85°F.). The lower part of this range is suitable for the European species, while the upper is often necessary to maintain the appetite of young Red-eared Turtles.

It will take a few hours for the temperature of the tank to equilibrate, and then, once a final check has been made, particularly on the effectiveness of the thermostatically-controlled heating unit, the turtles can be released into the tank. The depth of water is not critical, but it should be at least 15 cm. (6 in.), so the turtles have plenty of room in which to swim.

Releasing the Newly Purchased Turtle

Many turtles are sold in plastic bags containing their tank water from the shop. On arrival home, this water will have chilled, and to

American River Turtle (*Podocnemis erythrocephala*).

43

protect them from a sudden rise in temperature, the bag should be floated in the new tank. The water in the bag will be warmed, rising gradually to the temperature of the tank. This may take fifteen minutes or so, and then the turtles can be allowed to enter their new environment. They should not be handled more than necessary, and can be restrained in a cupped hand rather than held tightly, particularly when young. Holding a young turtle with a finger on either side of the marginal shields can damage this soft part of the shell, leading to subsequent deformities.

Plants

Water plants usually cannot be established in a tank containing turtles. The active nature of these reptiles does not give plants any opportunity to develop a system of roots. In addition, many turtles will also consume a certain amount of greenstuff as part of their diet and so damage any plants which do become established. Small pieces of washed watercress can be dropped into a tank and are

a useful addition to the diet, but they should be removed at frequent intervals as they turn yellow. The oxygen content of the aquarium water is much less important for turtles than for fish, as they rely mainly on the atmosphere for their supply of this gas.

Tank Cleanliness

The tank will need to be cleaned out very frequently perhaps every other day, if there is no filter in their tank. The situation is worsened if they are also being fed in the same environment, as the water will then rapidly be fouled by the remains of the food, as well as their excrement.

Filters

There are now very efficient filters which can be obtained, and when using a separate tank for feeding purposes, the main tank may only need to be cleaned every three months or so. Good hygiene is important because the fouled water is a potential reservoir for human infections, as well as endangering the turtles' health.

An aquarist shop will be able to advise on the filters

available, but generally undergravel filters are not as efficient for turtles as those located actually in the tank water. The best option in many cases is an internal power filter. It consists of a combined pump and filter unit which comprises an outer case and an inner cartridge of foam. The debris is sucked in and held on the foam cartridge, which is simply washed off or replaced at intervals as required.

The tank requires very little attention under these circumstances, apart from topping up the water level to replace the water which has evaporated. The filter should, if possible, be located under the stones at one end of the tank, because it is here that the majority of the debris will collect. The power filter is safe to use in a tank with even the smallest of turtles and is just as effective with larger individuals.

Emptying the Tank

There are times when the tank will need to be emptied completely, and this can be a problem because of the weight of water it contains. The water itself can be bailed out with an old tin or jug, or siphoned off using a length of rubber tubing; this should be filled with water, and

Mediterranean Spur-thighed Tortoise (*Testudo graeca*) parent with young. This species is also known as the Iberian Tortoise.

then one end is inserted into the tank, while the other is quickly lowered into a bucket positioned at a lower level than the tank. *The tank water must never be sucked initially by mouth through the tube, because of the potential disease hazard.* The gravel and stones can then be cleaned thoroughly, before being returned to the tank. Alternatively, you can buy a special siphon from an aquarist store.

Wintering

In the winter, the turtles will need to be brought inside, unless there is sufficient mud for them to hibernate in on the floor of the pond. They require a minimum depth of about 30 cm. (1 ft.) of mud in which to burrow, while the water itself should be at least 60 cm. (2 ft.) deep. Large turtles can be hibernated successfully like tortoises. In a box, however, they are more active at first than tortoises and need to be inspected regularly until they settle down, in case they roll over onto their backs and become trapped in this position.

As with tortoises, however,

it is not essential for turtles to hibernate, and it is often safer to keep them awake in an indoor tank for the winter months. When the temperature outside rises, they can be reacclimatized and placed back in their pond. If there is any risk of frost, the turtles will need to be brought back inside each evening and kept in unheated surroundings.

Sunlight and Exercise

Although only large specimens of the hardy species can be kept outside for much of the year, all turtles derive great benefit from sunlight. On fine days, they should be placed outside in a smaller tank containing a rock so they are able to bask in the sun. This ensures that they receive sufficient natural ultra-violet light to synthesize their own vitamin D_3, and will also serve to stimulate their appetites. The tank should be uncovered, because unfortunately glass tends to filter out this component of sunlight. As always, the turtles should not be exposed to the direct rays of the sun at its hottest, or the temperature of their surroundings will soon reach a high level. The critical upper temperature for most reptiles is just over 39°C. (100°F.), and exposure to temperatures above this figure is rapidly fatal for them.

Most turtles in the wild spend a fair amount of time out of the water, walking short distances over land. When kept constantly in a tank they are deprived of such exercise, and their muscles suffer as a result, so they can have great difficulty in walking on land. A regular supervised period enabling the turtles to walk outside their tank is to be recommended.

Feeding

Incorrect feeding is the major cause of mortality in young turtles. These reptiles normally take a wide range of foods in the wild, and adequate variety must be offered to captive individuals. A varied selection is important in maintaining a turtle's appetite, and apart from meat and fish in various forms, some vegetable matter should also be provided.

Young turtles, especially when first obtained, may be reluctant to eat, but most can be tempted immediately by livefood. Small tubifex worms available from many aquarist shops are popular and may be kept for a few days in a cool spot until required, if the water in their jar is changed daily. Daphnia and other crustaceans will appeal particularly to small turtles, while a culture of whiteworms is a useful standby if other livefoods are in short supply, as happens from time to time. In addition they will not introduce disease, as can happen with livefoods of aquatic origin.

False Map Turtle, *Graptemys pseudogeographica.* **Wonder if he knows his way home?**

Breeding Whiteworms

Several margarine tubs with lids make ideal breeding containers for whiteworms. They need to be filled with several inches of light loam soil which must be kept moist but never flooded. The initial supply of worms is divided between the tubs, and food such as brown bread soaked in milk is placed with them on the soil surface. The lid will help to retain the moisture within. The medium should be kept in a temperature of about 20°C. (70°F.), which is ideal for their breeding cycle. Worms should be taken from each culture in turn, so their numbers can recover in between, and those fed can be dusted with a vitamin and mineral powder beforehand.

Fish

Most people dislike the idea of feeding live fish such as guppies (*Poecilia reticulata*) to their turtles, and indeed this is not necessary, although some fish should be included regularly in their diet. Fresh small fish can be fed whole and uncooked to larger turtles but will need to be cut into sections for small

individuals. Such fish are an important source of vitamin A and so help to prevent eye problems which are sadly common in young terrapins. Raw herring is also popular and can be fed whole, complete with heads. Excessive feeding of fish is likely to be harmful though, as with all foodstuffs of this type.

Meat

Raw lean minced meat cut into small pieces is also suitable for feeding, and should be sprinkled with a vitamin and mineral preparation or powdered cuttlefish bone as necessary. Liver is best avoided, because the calcium: phosphorus ratio, being about 1:50, is too high; the imbalance between these two minerals will lead to soft and deformed shells. Heart should not be fed for the same reason, but other meats are generally quite suitable.

Additional Foods

Various terrestrial invertebrates will often be eaten by captive turtles. Snails, woodlice and small earthworms are all acceptable but must be

obtained from land which is not treated with an insecticide of any kind. Greenfood as fed to tortoises can also be offered to turtles but is best cut into small pieces beforehand. Such variety is vital for keeping these reptiles in good health, and some experimentation within reason is likely to prove beneficial. Large turtles will even take canned dog or cat food, but this should be given in moderation if liver and heart form the bulk of the brand concerned.

Special complete diets for turtles in the form of pellets are now the most satisfactory means of feeding these reptiles. They will provide all the necessary nutrients and usually prove quite palatable, even to smaller individuals. In addition, the excrement of turtles being fed on a diet of this type is easily dealt with by a power filter and does not soil the water in the tank as readily as that produced by turtles being fed a meat or fish-based diet. Check, however, that the brand you use is a *complete* food. Dried foods for turtles have a bad reputation in some quarters. In some instances this is still justified, since they are of no real nutritional value and, indeed, are not taken by the turtles concerned. Pelleted diets for fish can be used, but palatability varies from brand to brand in this case.

The Feeding Regimen

This will vary somewhat, depending on the foodstuff concerned, but generally,

49

turtles need to be fed on a daily basis, particularly when first obtained. Once they reach a size of 5 cm. (2 in.) they can be fed six days out of every seven, and this should help to maintain their appetites. The turtles will soon come to recognize feeding time, and many can be tamed without difficulty to take food from the hand. This is particularly useful when feeding meat or fish dusted with a supplement or powdered cuttlefish bone, as the supplement is less likely to be washed off in the water. The majority of turtles feed underwater, but some will occasionally take small invertebrates on land when out of their tank.

Using a Feeding Tank

It is useful to be able to transfer the turtle to a separate tank, containing water of the same temperature, for feeding purposes. Since they will rapidly consume their food and need only be out of their main tank for about half an hour, there is no need to keep this water heated. A few turtles resent such movement, however, and have to be fed in their usual

50

surroundings. This seems to apply particularly to the Pancake Turtles (*Trionyx* species), which spend much of their time buried on the floor of their aquarium.

There are several advantages of using a different tank or even a clean bowl for feeding times. It obviously helps to reduce fouling in the main tank. A close watch can be kept to ensure that all individuals are eating satisfactorily, while nervous and smaller individuals can be isolated from bigger turtles when being fed. Injuries are less likely at feeding time, when large specimens in particular may snap indiscriminately at anything which resembles food, including the limbs and tail of small turtles. Furthermore, in a mixed group some species will be less keen to eat at first than others, and so should be fed separately. The amount of food consumed at one sitting is obviously variable, depending on the numbers and size of the turtles, but they can be fed until they are no longer hungry. Young specimens will benefit from being offered smaller quantities several times a day. The use of a calcium supplement is of great importance for growing turtles.

Breeding

The breeding behavior of turtles is similar to that of tortoises, with courtship being a violent procedure. The male circles his intended mate in the water, with his head bobbing up and down. After mounting, the male remains firmly clasped to the female by means of his claws and will frequently bite her neck. They swim for a while in this position, the female having to force herself up to the surface for air. The resulting oval eggs are then laid on land and buried like those of a tortoise. The European Pond Turtle lays about ten eggs in a clutch averaging about 2.5 cm. (1 in.) in size, as do the sliders.

Mating is quite often seen in captive individuals from the age of five years onwards, but since few have access to an area of soil for laying purposes, even fewer actual breedings are recorded in the home. The first sign that a captive individual is laying will probably be the broken remains of an egg in the tank. Turtles living outside in a pond are more likely to breed, as they have access to areas of suitable terrain for egg-laying. A box filled with a mixture of sand and earth and built into the design of the tank platform may prove acceptable to those kept indoors.

The eggs should be treated as described for tortoises, with the surface of the box moistened every day using a fine spray of warm water. Any youngsters which hatch can be reared in an identical manner to other young bought from a store.

Growth and Aging

As might be expected, young turtles grow rapidly in their first years and then their growth rate gradually slows down. The growth rings, less obvious in turtles than tortoises, again reflect a season's growth and need not coincide with an annual pattern. Size is obviously influenced by a range of factors, including feeding, and while no definite guidelines can be laid down, providing the reptile appears healthy and is eating well there need be no cause for concern.

Health Problems

Tortoises and aquatic turtles are not difficult creatures to maintain in good health, providing their environmental needs for warmth and light are fully considered. Regular feeding and cleanliness will then eliminate the risk of most common health problems before they can develop, once the reptiles are established in their surroundings. Newly acquired chelonians are more likely to be a source of worry for their owners, however, and should always be kept isolated from others for a time, in case they are carrying a disease which could prove infectious. Appetite is a good indication of chelonian health. Once the new arrivals have eaten well during several days, they can be introduced to their companions.

Chelonian Medicine

Minor health problems can often be dealt with by the owner, but it will be necessary on occasion to seek veterinary advice. Although not all veterinarians have a great deal of experience with chelonians as patients, they are in a position to contact others with more specialized knowledge in this field for further advice if necessary. Routine tests, for example on a fecal sample for a possible intestinal worm infection, can also be undertaken speedily and reliably with the help of a veterinarian. Research into the diseases of chelonians is constantly adding to existing knowledge. For example, a *Herpes* virus belonging to the same group as those which cause cold sores in humans has been identified recently as a reason for sudden deaths in turtles.

Many of the techniques used routinely for the treatment of domestic dogs and cats can also be applied successfully to chelonians, providing veterinary advice is sought without delay when the reptile first appears ill. X-rays can be used for diagnostic purposes, and there are now anesthetics which enable surgery to be carried out safely and effectively on reptiles, including chelonians.

Modern drugs including antibiotics are available for treatment and can be given orally or by injection. The top of a back leg is usually the site for such injections, which are preferred because absorption of the antibiotic is generally more effective. Calculations of dosage are often based on "soft-weight," which is the total weight of the chelonian minus a third, to take into account the weight of its shell. It is therefore useful to know the reptile's weight when consulting a veterinarian, and regular weighing aids as a useful health check.

There is no excuse for not seeking advice on chelonians or other reptiles if they are ill on the grounds that nothing can be done for them. In hopeless cases, the creature can be destroyed painlessly with veterinary assistance. Apart from sentimental value, the expense of treatment is often justified simply by the cost of

Two-headed Painted Turtle (Chrysemys picta marginata). Two-headed turtles are more commonly encountered than you might suppose.

purchasing another individual, particularly one of the rarer species.

Colds

This term is widely used to describe any infection of the airways, and chelonians like other animals can be afflicted with such complaints. The underlying cause may be a virus or a bacterium or often a mixture of both; a viral infection usually predisposes to a more severe secondary bacterial invasion. Fungal infections have also been reported, and one author suggests that these may be directly responsible for three per cent of the deaths of tortoises kept in captivity. Hay is a potential source of such infections and so must not be used for bedding purposes.

Symptoms

In tortoises, a discharge from the nostrils is often the first symptom of a respiratory disorder, while the eyes are also usually watery. If left untreated, the breathing will become labored and pneumonia may develop, with a fatal outcome.

Treatment

Raising the temperature of the tortoise's environment to 23°C. (75°F.) and keeping it indoors out of drafts should help to improve the condition. In mild cases a mentholated ointment available from pharmacists can be used. It must be smeared carefully around the jaws as directed on the pack, and the vapor will help to loosen the secretions. The nose should be wiped frequently and the eyes bathed as necessary. A wide variety of foodstuffs must be provided to encourage the patient to continue eating.

A veterinarian should be consulted for further advice if the tortoise does not improve rapidly. Antibiotic treatment will prove effective in many cases. If necessary, a swab of the nasal discharge can be submitted to a laboratory for tests. These should help to reveal the causal microorganism and the drug to which it is most susceptible. The tortoise will need to be kept inside until it has fully recovered and is eating well. Thereafter it must not be exposed to damp conditions and only allowed out during periods of fine weather.

Pneumonia in Turtles

Turtles can also be afflicted with similar respiratory infections, and those which swim with difficulty may be suffering from pneumonia. In cases where one lung primarily is affected, this side of the body is kept lower than the other so the turtle swims at an unusual angle. Dirty conditions predispose to infections of this kind, as harmful bacteria such as *Pseudomonas* will multiply rapidly in fouled water contaminated with decaying food.

Eye Ailments

Turtles, especially young Red-ears and related *Chrysemys* species, are susceptible to an eye complaint which affects the lids, leading to blindness. The minute Harderian glands, first identified in deer by the Swiss anatomist Harder in 1694, are the source of the problem. These are similar to the tear glands of humans and excrete excess salt from the body. This function is undertaken very efficiently by the human kidneys, so the Harderian glands are only rudimentary

Seychelles Giant Tortoise (*Geochelone gigantea*). This species has been rendered endangered by feral domestic animals and by humans, who hunt it for food.

"Turtles will often open their mouths if they are smeared with olive oil, and a small piece of food can be popped in on the end of a blunt cocktail stick."

in man. The reptilian kidney is not as well adapted, so these glands are particularly well developed in marine reptiles which have to cope with an increased burden of salt in their environment. In the diseased state, the normal structure of the glands is lost and they swell as keratin is laid down in them. This tough, fibrous protein occurs naturally in the skin, scales and claws. As a result, the eyelids become swollen, the change being noticeable initially in the upper lid. They fuse together, blinding the turtle completely, and it refuses to eat, eventually dying a week or two later. Both eyes are normally affected, but on rare occasions only one becomes sealed so that the reptile may continue eating.

Cause

The cause of this distressing condition appears to be a dietary deficiency of vitamin A, so the regular use of a suitable supplement on the food is recommended, especially if meat is being fed, since this tends to be low in vitamin A. Cod or other fish liver oils can also be given on food, but there are possible problems associated with feeding liver directly on a regular basis.

Treatment

Treatment of the condition, if it develops, is unlikely to be satisfactory in the latter stages, but two injections of vitamin A given at an interval of a week have effected a cure in some cases. It will also be necessary to feed the reptile by hand, which in itself is no easy task. Turtles will often open their mouths if they are smeared with olive oil, and a small piece of food can be popped in on the end of a blunt cocktail stick. The patient may then need to be put in water to swallow the mouthful, and the process repeated several times. This condition, without doubt, is more easily prevented than cured.

Bacterial Infections

Eye infections caused by bacteria are encountered occasionally in both tortoises and turtles. They can be treated simply by means of an antibiotic ophthalmic ointment applied to the eye as directed. Turtles should be kept out of water for at least fifteen minutes after treatment so that the drug has time to penetrate to the site of infection. In such cases, the eyeball itself is affected, whereas in the case of vitamin A deficiency it is not involved. Eye discharges can also accompany respiratory infections.

Fungus

Fungal infections have been reported in both tortoises and freshwater turtles but are very rare in marine species. *Aspergillus* has been identified in the lungs of tortoises. Overcrowding and poor husbandry are major factors in such cases. Infection occasionally even occurs on the carapace.

Fungus is most commonly seen in turtles, particularly newly acquired youngsters. The Pancake Turtles with their leathery shells appear most susceptible to fungal infections until they are established in their surroundings. Stress of any kind, therefore, particularly changes in temperature, is probably a major predisposing factor. Fungal growth gives the turtles a haloed effect over the body resembling fine cotton-wool, which is particularly obvious when they are in the water.

Treatment

Immersing the turtle in a salt solution, made with a quarter teaspoon of salt stirred into a cup of water at the correct temperature, for a quarter of an hour daily may prove effective. Fish fungus remedies can be used safely on turtles suffering from fungus, while various ointments which are applied directly can be obtained from a veterinarian.

Injuries

Small cuts on the limbs of tortoises should be cleaned and dabbed with a safe germicidal ointment. It may be necessary to cover the wound with a bandage, particularly if the reptile is being trouble by flies. More severe injuries, such as the loss of a limb, require similar treatment once they have begun to heal; there is no reason why a tortoise cannot live adequately on three functional limbs if a protective pad is placed on the remaining stump. This dressing should be changed at intervals as necessary. In the case of an infection, however, an antibiotic ointment must be obtained.

Damage to the shell may

"Fungal infections have been reported in both tortoises and freshwater turtles but are very rare in marine species . . . Overcrowding and poor husbandry are major factors in such cases."

arise during transit or can be caused by an accident at home. In many cases, even when the injury penetrates to the tissue itself, it is possible to repair the wound surgically under anesthesia. Fiberglass and epoxy resin, used primarily for patching the bodywork of cars, will form the seal on the shell once the vet has dealt with the underlying injury, enabling the bony fragments to heal underneath. Shell damage will be repaired slowly, over a period of years, rather than in days as with skin wounds.

Loss of Appetite

As an initial step to overcoming the problem of loss of appetite, the environmental temperature should be raised to 29°C. (85°F.) for turtles and at least 23°C. (75°F.) for tortoises. A variety of food is essential at this time, to restore a healthy appetite. Any illness, such as a mouth infection, will cause these reptiles to lose interest in food.

Newly imported tortoises are often very loathe to eat when they are first acquired. If they refuse all foods, then standing them in a shallow bowl of warm water with a temperature of about 23°C. (75°F.) for a quarter of an hour or so each day often proves effective. Food should be offered by hand at the same time. Once they start eating regularly, the problem rarely recurs. This method is also useful for individuals which are reluctant to feed after hibernation.

If, in spite of all attempts, the chelonian's appetite does not return naturally, then the animal should be taken to a veterinarian, who may advise giving a vitamin injection. As a last resort, it may then be necessary for the veterinarian to sedate the tortoise and feed it via a stomach-tube each day until it regains its strength. A small amount of liquid invalid food, about half a teaspoon (3 ml) is given by this means. It is possible to overfeed a tortoise artificially; those under approximately 1 kg (2.2 lb.) have a total stomach capacity of as little as 10 ml.

Mouth Infections

This problem is a relatively common condition in tortoises, and is often seen when they first awake after hibernation. The reptile will appear to have difficulty in eating its food, and close inspections will show that the inside of the mouth is ulcerated. The tortoise's head should be held carefully but firmly and the jaws gently pried open. There may be a discharge from around the lips, and even hemorrhage in some cases. It is a most unpleasant condition, with bacteria of the Gram-negative group being commonly isolated in such cases, perhaps with a fungal involvement as well.

Veterinary advice should be sought early if an infection of this type is suspected. Treatment, if practical, necessitates a course of antibiotic injections, while the inside of the mouth has to be cleaned and dressed with a safe disinfectant. Sedation will almost certainly be necessary, and the tortoise will have to be fed via a stomach-tube until it recovers.

Parasites

A wide range of chelonian parasites have been identified, including microscopic protozoa which live in the blood cells, but there are three types which are a major cause of concern to those who keep these reptiles. None, as far as known, is of any disease significance to humans.

Ticks

Ticks, normally the species known as *Hyalomma aegyptium*, occur on the vast majority of imported Greek tortoises and can be seen on the soft parts of the body. The immature stages of this tick are found on a wide

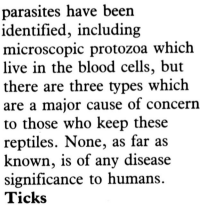

Frog-headed Turtle (*Phrynops nasuta wermuthi*), one of the Side-necks.

59

range of animals in the wild, including partridges, hares and mice, but the adult ticks are confined to tortoises and, occasionally hedgehogs.

It is this stage which is seen, as the immature larvae and nymphs are probably lost in transit. The brownish male ticks are more common than the larger whitish females, which can reach the size of a fingernail. These ticks, while they are feeding on the tortoise's blood, can transmit a protozoal coccidian parasite, *Haemogregarina*, which then invades the red blood cells of the reptile but does not appear to cause any significant harm.

Many dealers remove ticks before selling the tortoises, but some will slip through unnoticed. The inner regions of the thigh and the base of the neck are common sites; the thigh tubercle of the Spur-Thighed Tortoise should not be confused with a tick.

Most tropical ticks will eventually drop off, but it is generally preferable to remove them. This is easily accomplished by applying a little menthylated spirit to

Three-keeled Box Turtle (*Cuora trifasciata*). This species requires ample ultraviolet radiation in order to stay healthy.

the point where the tick is anchored; it should then release its grip slightly and can be pulled out cleanly with a suitable pair of tweezers. Pressure applied relatively close to the site of attachment is most effective in helping pull the tick out whole. On occasion, the head will be left buried in the tortoise's flesh, when the area should be dabbed with an ointment. For this reason it is often safer to cover the tick with petroleum jelly so that it drops off intact, being unable to breathe, rather than risk leaving its head behind, as this can set up a serious infection.

Salmonella

Salmonella infections are significant because they can spread from tortoises and terrapins to man. This is currently the only known disease which these reptiles can transmit to humans. The symptoms are usually those of food poisoning, but the danger is that an apparently healthy chelonian can carry these bacteria. Such affected individuals may be detected, however, by culturing for the bacteria from a fecal sample. A veterinarian can advise on this testing.

Painted Turtle (*Chrysemys picta picta*).

61

Children are particularly at risk if they are allowed close, unsupervised contact with these reptiles. Infection normally occurs by ingestion of the bacteria, so it is sensible to wash one's hands thoroughly, after having handled a tortoise or turtle, especially before eating or touching food. Gloves can be worn when cleaning out a tank, and all utensils kept apart from those used for domestic purposes.

In spite of the headlines which occasionally result when a case of food poisoning is traced back to the family tortoise, the actual chances of infection would appear relatively slight.

Shell Problems

Softening of the shell seen in chelonians kept indoors has two major causes. The sun's ultra-violet rays (filtered out by glass) are responsible for the natural production of vitamin D_3 by the body. This vitamin then acts to control the absorption and movement of calcium in particular, and a deficiency will interfere with the deposition of calcium. Young, growing animals of all species are especially at

risk, and the condition referred to as rickets soon develops. Cod liver oil is a valuable source of vitamin D and can be given on the food, but a wide-spectrum light or natural sunlight is preferable. A dietary excess of both vitamins A and D_3 can be harmful, so any tonics used must be given in the recommended dose.

A shortage of calcium, either direct or because the calcium:phosphorus ratio is too high, can also be responsible for soft shells. This is prevented by scraping cuttlefish bone onto the food or giving a soluble salt such as calcium lactate in a similar manner. Some owners leave a piece of cuttlefish bone floating in the turtle tank, so the reptiles can take it themselves, but few seem to respond in this way.

Algal growth on the shells of older turtles need not give cause for concern. Shedding of the complete shell shields of *Chrysemys* turtles is also a natural phenomenon. These must not be pulled off when they start to peel, as this may result in injury.

Kept under satisfactory

conditions, a chelonian's lifespan should be measured in decades, making them potentially the most long-lived of all animals kept as pets. Owning a chelonian is a truly rewarding experience.

Female Green Turtle (*Chelonia mydas*) returning to the sea after laying her eggs.

Index

Argentine (Chaco) Tortoise, 23
Bacterial infections, 56
Bell's Hingeback, 24
Blanding's Turtle, 30
Box Turtles, 26–28
Brown Tortoise, 26
Calcium, 17, 62
Caspian Turtle, 31
Chrysemys, 32–34
Chrysemys concinna, 33
Chrysemys floridana, 33
Chrysemys picta, 34
Chrysemys rubriventris, 33
Chrysemys (Pseudemys) scripta elegans, 32
Chrysemys scripta scripta, 32
Colds, 54
Cuora, 28
Dermochelys coriacea, 4
Diamondback, 36
Eastern (Common) Box Turtle, 27
Emydoidea blandingi, 30
Emys, 30
Emys orbicularis, 30
Eroded Hingeback, 24
False Map (Sawback) Turtle, 37
Florida Cooter, 33
Fungus, 57
Geochelone carbonaria, 22
Geochelone chilensis, 23
Geochelone dentriculata, 23
Geochelone elegans, 26
Geochelone elephantopus, 3
Geochelone elongata, 25
Geochelone emys, 26
Geochelone gigantea, 3
Geochelone pardalis, 24
Geochelone sulcata, 24
Giant Tortoise, 3
Gopherus, 26
Graptemys pseudogeographica, 37
Growth, 22, 51
Harderian glands, 55
Hermann's (Greek) Tortoise, 6
Hibernation, 20–22, 40
Home's Hingeback, 24
Housing, 10–15, 39–42
Injuries, 57

Kinixys belliani, 24
Kinixys erosa, 24
Kinixys homeana, 24
Kinosternon, 34
Leatherback, 4
Leopard Tortoise, 24
Malaclemys terrapin, 36
Malacochersus tornieri, 24
Margined Tortoise, 8
Mauremys caspica, 31
Mauremys leprosa, 31
Mediterranean Spur-thighed Tortoise, 6
Mouth infections, 58
Mud Turtles, 34
Musk Turtle, 34
Ornate Box Turtle, 28
Painted Turtle, 34
Pancake Tortoise, 24
Pancake (Soft-shelled) Turtles, 36
Parasites, 59
Pond Turtles, 30
Red-bellied Slider, 33
Red-eared Turtle, 32
Red-footed Tortoise, 22
Salmonella, 61
Shell problems, 62
Spanish Turtle, 31
Spurred Tortoise, 24
Starred Tortoise, 26
Sternotherus, 34
Terrapene carolina, 27
Terrapene carolina bauri, 27
Terrapene carolina triunguis, 27
Terrapene coahuila, 28
Terrapene nelsoni, 28
Testudo graeca, 6
Testudo hermanni, 6
Testudo marginata, 8
Texas Slider, 33
Ticks, 59
Triassochelys, 2
Trionyx, 36
Water, 17, 43
Yellow Tortoise, 25
Yellow-bellied Turtle, 32
Yellow-footed Tortoise, 23

Parrot-beaked Tortoise (*Homopus areolatus*). Photo by Dr. Herbert R. Axelrod.